How To Use This Study Guide

This five-lesson study guide corresponds to *"Pulling Down Strongholds" With Rick Renner* (**Renner TV**). Each lesson in this study guide covers a topic that is addressed during the program series, with questions and references supplied to draw you deeper into your own private study of the Scriptures on this subject.

To derive the most benefit from this study guide, consider the following:

First, watch or listen to the program prior to working through the corresponding lesson in this guide. (Programs can also be viewed at **renner.org** by clicking on the Media/Archives links.)

Second, take the time to look up the scriptures included in each lesson. Prayerfully consider their application to your own life.

Third, use a journal or notebook to make note of your answers to each lesson's Study Questions and Practical Application challenges.

Fourth, invest specific time in prayer and in the Word of God to consult with the Holy Spirit. Write down the scriptures or insights He reveals to you about being filled with the Spirit and empowered by Him in your daily life.

Finally, take action! Whatever the Lord tells you to do according to His Word, do it.

For added insights on this subject, it is recommended that you obtain Rick Renner's book *Dressed To Kill: A Biblical Approach to Spiritual Warfare and Armor.* You may also select from Rick's other available resources by placing your order at **renner.org** or by calling 1-800-742-5593.

TOPIC

What Is a Stronghold?

SCRIPTURES

1. **2 Corinthians 10:4** — For the weapons of our warfare are not carnal, but mighty through God to the pulling down of strong holds.

GREEK WORDS

1. "pulling down" — **καθαιρέω** (*kathaireo*): to take down; to disassemble, if needed, bit by bit; to demolish; to destroy; to dismantle; to throw down; to knock down, break up, pull apart, and take to pieces until nothing is left standing; used to picture pulling down the walls of a well-defended fortress

2. "strongholds" — **ὀχύρωμα** (*ochuroma*): fortress; castle; citadel; pictures a stronghold with walls fortified to keep outsiders on the outside; a dreadful prison constructed deep inside a fortress that was intended to prevent a hostage or prisoner from escaping; a place of arrest, captivity, confinement, detention, imprisonment, or incarceration

SYNOPSIS

The five lessons in this study on *Pulling Down Strongholds* will focus on the following topics:

- What Is a Stronghold?
- Weapons To Demolish a Mental Stronghold
- Logical and Illogical Strongholds
- Bringing Every Thought Into Captivity
- How To Help Others Get Free From Mental Strongholds

The emphasis of this lesson:

A stronghold is a fortress of lies the enemy builds in your mind and emotions. It is a place of arrest, captivity, confinement, detention,

imprisonment, or incarceration in your thinking that prevents you from experiencing all God has planned for your life.

Since the beginning of recorded history, people have built walls around their cities to serve as barriers of protection from enemy forces. In most cases, these walls were high, thick, and impenetrable. We see an example of such fortifications standing in downtown Moscow today. Amazingly, these walls were built between 1535 and 1538 — nearly 500 years ago — to serve as a stronghold of protection for the citizens of the city.

What is interesting is the same walls that keep out an enemy invasion can also serve to imprison those who are inside. And what is true in the natural realm is also true in the realm of the spirit. Satan, the enemy of your soul, is always seeking an opportunity to gain entrance into your life and erect a *stronghold*. Thankfully, you don't have to be imprisoned by his lies. You can learn how to recognize strongholds and pull them down with the spiritual weapons God has given you!

What Is a Stronghold?

The classic biblical text on the subject of strongholds is found in Second Corinthians 10:4. It says, "For the weapons of our warfare are not carnal, but mighty through God to the pulling down of *strong holds.*" The Greek word for "strongholds" here is the word *ochuroma*, and it describes *a fortress, a castle,* or *a citadel.* It pictures *a stronghold with walls fortified to keep outsiders on the outside.* At the same time, it depicts *a dreadful prison constructed deep inside a fortress that was intended to prevent a hostage or prisoner from escaping.* Thus, a stronghold is *a place of arrest, captivity, confinement, detention, imprisonment,* or *incarceration.*

In a spiritual sense, a stronghold is any lie you are believing that imprisons you. As we will see in the lessons ahead, the enemy is very strategic and persistent in his efforts to construct a stronghold. Little by little, he stealthily presents you with a lie here and a deception there — again and again and again. Each lie you believe becomes another brick in the wall of the stronghold he is attempting to construct. Although you can't see or touch the imaginary prison bars, they are there holding you hostage to ideas and imaginations that have no basis in reality.

So when you read Paul's words about strongholds in Second Corinthians 10:4, you need to see it as both a *fortress* and a *prison* in your mind and then apply that picture to your own life. Are their areas in your mind and emotions that are currently being influenced or controlled by the enemy's lies of fear, doubt, and worry? Do you find yourself repeatedly being attacked in the same areas? Do you feel like a prisoner to these areas of your mind and emotions? If you answered yes to any of these questions, you have probably allowed the enemy to construct a stronghold in your mind and emotions and it is hindering you from stepping out to fulfill God's call on your life.

Our Self-Image Is a Prime Target

One of the areas Satan attempts to build strongholds in our lives is in how we see and think of ourselves. We can see this clearly in the examples Rick shared from his life.

When he was a boy, he was never into sports, yet they seemed to dominate the landscape of his life. Softball, basketball, and bowling were a regular part of his family and church life. Fishing was also a favorite pastime of his father that he participated in, but he really had no interest in it. To him, these things seemed like drudgery and a waste of time. From the earliest of ages, Rick enjoyed things like going to the symphony, visiting the museum, and painting outdoor landscape portraits.

Clearly, he was programmed differently and was quite unique from those around him, which is normal and to be expected. But over time he began to think something was really wrong with him. The enemy capitalized on this disparity at an early age and began feeding him thoughts like, *What is wrong with me? Why am I so strange? Why am I such a freak?*

Then in the seventh grade, after getting severely sick in school and missing about half the year, he returned to his classes only to find that he was way behind in his subjects. When the teachers presented the material, he felt as though they were speaking a foreign language, and no one took the time to help bring him up to speed with the rest of the class. Again, thoughts and feelings of inferiority swirled within his mind, and the enemy began to tell him, "You're just stupid."

By the ninth grade, not only was Rick hearing the "I am stupid" recording playing in his brain, his teacher also began calling him "stupid" daily in front of the entire class. On top of all this, Rick tested poorly on a job placement exam that same year. When the job placement counselors called him in to go over his performance, they told him to never attempt higher education because he was not mentally equipped for that type of learning. "Learn how to use a shovel or pour concrete," they said. "Manual labor is really all you're cut out for."

Again and again and again, the enemy fired his lies at Rick's mind from seemingly every angle. He strategically used his classmates and people in authority to hammer home his messages of deception. More and more, Rick was beginning to believe he was inferior, defective, and stupid. But before his self-image was destroyed, God lovingly baptized Rick in the Holy Spirit, and he was totally set free!

You Can 'Pull Down' the Enemy's Strongholds

Make no mistake: the devil wants to take you out. Although he is not all-knowing, he is well aware that God has a good plan for your life and wants to use you to advance His Kingdom. When the Kingdom of God advances, the kingdom of darkness declines and suffers defeat. Satan knows that and seeks to stop you from living out your divine destiny. Hence, he seeks to inundate and penetrate your mind and emotions with false information to establish his strongholds.

Thankfully, you don't have to live incarcerated within his prison. You can break free! God has given you weapons! Again, the Bible says, "For the weapons of our warfare are not carnal, but mighty through God to the pulling down of strong holds" (2 Corinthians 10:4). The words "pulling down" in Greek is *kathaireo*, which means *to take down* or *to disassemble, if needed, bit by bit or piece by piece.* It can also be translated *to demolish; to destroy; to dismantle;* or *to throw down.* It carries such force that it means *to knock down, break up, pull apart, and take to pieces until nothing is left standing.* The word *kathaireo* is used to picture pulling down the walls of a well-defended fortress.

When you dismantle a house brick by brick, it can be very tedious and seem like it is taking forever. But if you faithfully keep swinging your hammer, eventually you will dismantle it. The same commitment and persistence is needed for pulling down strongholds in your life. Make up your mind that you are going to knock them down, break them up, and tear them apart bit-by-bit if needed until nothing is left standing in your life. In our next lesson, we will examine seven specific weapons God has given you to pull down Satan's strongholds.

STUDY QUESTIONS

**Study to shew thyself approved unto God, a workman that
needeth not to be ashamed, rightly dividing the word of truth.
— 2 Timothy 2:15**

1. When Jesus was in the desert fasting for 40 days, Satan attacked His identity (*see* Matthew 4:1-11). Likewise, he attacked Christ's identity when He was dying on the Cross (*see* Matthew 27:40-43). In what ways has the enemy attacked your identity? How did Jesus defeat the devil's lies in the desert? Are there any scriptures that come to mind that refute these lies?

2. The best way to destroy a lie is to *know the truth*. God says many things about you in His Word. Take time to look up these verses, and write out who He declares you to be in Christ.

   • **2 Corinthians 5:17** – God says I am _____

   _____.

   • **2 Corinthians 5:21** – God says I am _____

   _____.

   • **Romans 8:1** (John 3:18) – God says I am not _____

   _____.

   • **Ephesians 1:7** – God says I am _____

   _____.

   • **Ephesians 2:4-6** – God says I am _____

   _____.

   • **1 John 3:1, 2** – God says I am _____

   _____.

PRACTICAL APPLICATION

**But be ye doers of the word, and not hearers only,
deceiving your own selves.
—James 1:22**

1. In your own words, how would you describe a *stronghold*?

2. Rick candidly shared his testimony of how the enemy attempted to build a stronghold of worthlessness in his life. In what ways is your story similar to his story?

3. Satan not only attempts to lie to you about your self-image, but he also attempts to lie to you about God's image. In what specific ways has the enemy tried to twist and distort the image of God in your mind? What scriptures can you think of that refute these lies? (If need be, get a Bible concordance and begin looking up key words related to the truth about God that refutes the enemy's assertions.)

TOPIC

Weapons To Demolish a Mental Stronghold

SCRIPTURES

1. **2 Corinthians 10:4, 5** — For the weapons of our warfare are not carnal, but mighty through God to the pulling down of strong holds. Casting down imaginations, and every high thing that exalteth itself against the knowledge of God...

2. **Acts 10:38** — How God anointed Jesus of Nazareth with the Holy Ghost and with power: who went about doing good, and healing all that were oppressed of the devil; for God was with him.

3. **Ephesians 6:14-18** — Stand therefore, having your loins girt about with truth, and having on the breastplate of righteousness; and your feet shod with the preparation of the gospel of peace. Above all, taking the shield of faith, wherewith ye shall be able to quench all the fiery darts of the wicked. And take the helmet of salvation, and the sword of the Spirit, which is the word of God. Praying always with all prayer and supplication in the Spirit..."

GREEK WORDS

1. "strongholds" — ὀχύρωμα (*ochuroma*): fortress; castle; citadel; pictures a stronghold with walls fortified to keep outsiders on the outside; a dreadful prison constructed deep inside a fortress that was intended to prevent a hostage or prisoner from escaping; a place of arrest, captivity, confinement, detention, imprisonment, or incarceration

2. "oppressed"— **καταδυναστεύω** (*katadunasteuo*): a compound of **κατα** (*kata*) and **δυνάστης** (*dunastes*); the word **κατα** (*kata*) carries the idea of domination; the word **δυνάστης** (*dunastes*) depicts a dominating tyrant; when compounded, it pictures a wicked tyrant who rules over his subjects; bullying; cruelty; despotism; dictatorship; oppressiveness; tyranny

3. "devil"— **διάβολος** (*diabolos*): one who repetitiously strikes until successfully penetrating an object to ruin it, affect it, or take it captive; to slander, accuse, or defame; to penetrate by continuous assault; to ensnare with a net

4. "weapons"— **ὅπλα** (*hopla*): from **ὅπλον** (*hoplon*), armor, weapons; used in Ephesians 6:14-18 to depict the whole armor of God that potentially belongs to every believer

5. "whole armor"— **πανοπλία** (*panoplia*): from **πᾶν** and **ὅπλον** (*hoplon*);the whole armor or weapons belonging to a combat soldier

6. "wiles"— **μεθοδεία** (*methodeia*): from **μετά** (*meta*) and **ὁδός** (*hodos*); the word **μετά** (*meta*) means "with"; the word **ὁδός** (*hodos*) means "a road"; compounded, pictures one who travels on or operates on a specific road or avenue; carries the ideas of direction, plan, and purpose

7. "warfare"— **στρατεία** (*strateia*): a well-planned attack; derived from **στρατεύομαι** (*strateuomai*), which depicts strategic warfare; methods to be used in an attack and the route chosen to carry out a debilitating assault

8. "carnal"— **σαρκικός** (*sarkikos*): fleshly; natural; whatever is derived from the fleshly, natural, or material world

9. "mighty"— **δυνατὰ** (*dunata*): from **δύναμις** (*dunamis*), power; pictures explosive, superhuman power that comes with enormous energy and produces phenomenal, extraordinary, and unparalleled results; used to depict the full might and power of an advancing army

10. "through God"— **τῷ Θεῷ** (*to Theo*): through God; through the instrumentality of God; through a partnership with God

11. "pulling down"— **καθαιρέω** (*kathaireo*): to take down; to disassemble, if needed, bit by bit; to demolish; to destroy; to dismantle; to throw down; to knock down, break up, pull apart, and take to pieces until nothing is left standing; used to picture pulling down the walls of a well-defended fortress

SYNOPSIS

If you visit downtown Moscow today, you will find an area of the city known as Kitay-gorod. It is one of the oldest districts in Moscow where a number of very wealthy people once lived. Between the years of 1535 and 1538, the mother of Ivan the Terrible ordered that a series of connecting walls be erected to protect the people in this affluent section of the city. When this stronghold was completed, its walls were as wide as they were high. In fact, they were so wide that a chariot and a carriage with horses could run along its top. Throughout the nearly 500 hundred years of its existence, these walls effectively kept all outsiders from getting in, and at the same time, they kept those on the inside from getting out.

This ancient stronghold is an example of what many people — including believers — are dealing with in their mind and emotions. Little by little over an extended period of time, the enemy deceives people into accepting his lies about themselves, about God, and about life. As a result, he establishes strongholds in their thinking from which he begins to exert his influence and control over their lives.

The emphasis of this lesson:

According to Ephesians 6:14-18, we have been given seven spiritual weapons with which to defeat the enemy. Only by putting on the whole armor of God can we effectively stand against the devil's strategies and demolish any strongholds he has built in our lives.

Strongholds Act as Both a *Fortress* and a *Prison*

Thankfully, the Lord in His mercy has given us weapons to demolish the enemy's strongholds. The apostle Paul wrote about these weapons in Second Corinthians 10:4, declaring, "For the weapons of our warfare are not carnal, but mighty through God to the pulling down of strong holds."

As we learned in our first lesson, the word "stronghold" in Second Corinthians 10:4 comes from the Greek word *ochuroma*, and it describes *a fortress, a castle,* or a *citadel.* It pictures *a stronghold with walls fortified to keep outsiders on the outside.* Spiritually speaking, if a person has a stronghold, they are insulated by some kind of mental or emotional lie acting as a walled fortress in their soul. And the people who could help or would want to help are unable to penetrate the fortified walls surrounding them.

In addition to being a *fortress*, the word *ochuroma* — translated here as "stronghold" — also describes *a dreadful prison constructed deep inside a fortress that was intended to prevent a hostage or prisoner from escaping.* Thus, it is *a place of arrest, captivity, confinement, detention, imprisonment,* or *incarceration.* Essentially, a stronghold is formed when false information is believed to be true again and again and again. Every time a lie is received and believed, the invisible walls of a stronghold are strengthened.

Understanding How the Devil Operates

Before we go further, it is important for you to see the connection between the enemy's efforts to build strongholds in your life and Jesus' ministry of deliverance. Acts 10:38 says, "...God anointed Jesus of Nazareth with the Holy Ghost and with power: who went about doing good, and healing all that were oppressed of the devil; for God was with him." Note the word "oppressed" in this passage. It is the Greek word *katadunasteuo*, which is a compound of the words *kata* and *dunastes*. The word *kata* carries the idea of *domination*; the word *dunastes* depicts *a dominating tyrant.* When these words are compounded to form the word *katadunasteuo*, it pictures *a wicked tyrant who rules over his subjects.* This word can also be translated *bullying; cruelty; despotism; dictatorship; oppressiveness;* or *tyranny.*

Who is the tyrant referred to in this verse? It is the "devil," which is the Greek word *diabolos.* It is a compound of the word *dia*, which carries the idea of being *penetrated from one side all the way to the other side;* and the word *balos*, which means *to strike and strike repeatedly.* When *dia* and *balos* are joined together to form the word *diabolos*, it is a picture of *one who repetitiously strikes until successfully penetrating an object to ruin it, affect it, or take it captive.* It can also mean *to slander, accuse,* or *defame; to penetrate by continuous assault;* or *to ensnare with a net.*

If you think about it, the word *diabolos* is more of the devil's job description than it is his name. It tells us that when he strikes the mind and emotions, he doesn't just strike once. He strikes again and again and again — attacking the mind and attacking the emotions from every possible angle in order to ensnare it, penetrate it, and ruin it. If we believe the devil's lies, we give them power. Our faith always empowers what we believe. But we do not have to submit to his attacks.

The Seven Phases of Establishing a Stronghold

In the devil's attempts to establish a stronghold, there are seven major stages or phases.

Phase One
First, he personally brings an attack against your mind and emotions.

Phase Two
He then brings in reinforcements to support the mental and emotional attack with their words and actions. This would include people in authority as well as those you are close to in life.

Phase Three
In addition to phases one and two, life experiences begin to fortify the enemy's lie.

Phase Four
Influential voices can be used to bolster the intensity of the attack, as they yield to saying the same thing out loud that the devil has been speaking internally in your mind.

Phase Five
At this point, the concert of voices leads you to begin releasing *negative faith* in the lie. That is, you really begin to believe the lie that has been repeatedly spoken about you and is working in your mind and emotions.

Phase Six
In the sixth phase, the lie begins to transition from the mental realm into the physical and material realm of reality.

Phase Seven
The stronghold has been built, and the enemy takes you hostage. Like a wicked tyrant, he begins to rule over you and dominate your life. The ungodly thinking or behavior has become so ingrained in your brain that it is now a natural, seemingly effortless response.

Put on Your Spiritual Armor and Guard Your Mind

Looking at Second Corinthians 10:4, our foundational verse, it says, "For the weapons of our warfare are not carnal, but mighty through God to the pulling down of strong holds." Notice the word "weapons." It is the Greek word *hopla*, which is from the word *hoplon*, and it describes *armor* or *weapons*. It is the word used in Ephesians 6:14-18 to depict *the whole armor of God that potentially belongs to every believer*.

Just before the apostle Paul named each piece of the believer's armor, he wrote and said, "Put on the whole armour of God, that ye may be able to stand against the wiles of the devil" (Ephesians 6:11). The words "whole armour" is the Greek word *panoplia*, which is from the words *pan* and *hoplon* (the same word used in Second Corinthians 10:4). The word *pan* means *all*, and the word *hoplon* means *the whole armor or weapons belonging to a Roman combat soldier*. This is important to note as it reveals that God didn't give you just a few pieces of weaponry; He gave you *everything* that you need to deal with and defeat the enemy.

Also notice the word "wiles." It is the Greek word *methodeia*, which is a compound of the words *meta* and *hodos*. The word *meta* means *with*, and the word *hodos* means *a road*. When compounded, the new word *methodeia* pictures *one who travels on or operates on a specific road or avenue*. It carries the idea of a *direction*, *plan*, and *purpose*. This informs us that the devil is not traveling randomly; he has a specific avenue and purpose for his attack. He is heading straight for your mind because he knows that whoever controls your mind is going to control you. Your mind is the control center of your life.

Think about it. Whoever controls your mind will also control your emotions. And whoever controls your emotions can begin to affect your self-image, determine what you project to others, and manipulate you in any direction they desire. Again, the mind is the control center of your life. This is why Jesus wants to be Lord of your mind and He urges you to renew your mind with His Word. A mind that is swept and clean, yet absent of the truth of God's Word, is highly vulnerable to the enemy's strongholds.

Whose "wiles" are we talking about? The "devil's, which is once again the Greek word *diabalos*, meaning *one who repetitiously strikes until successfully penetrating an object to ruin it, affect it, or take it captive*. The target Satan and his forces repetitiously strike is your mind.

Seven Weapons With Which to Defeat the Devil

After Paul instructed us to "Put on the whole armour of God, that [we] may be able to stand against the wiles of the devil" (Ephesians 6:11), he then named seven specific pieces of weaponry God has given us with which to defend ourselves and fight the enemy.

In Ephesians 6:14, Paul wrote, "Stand therefore, having your loins girt about with truth, and having on the breastplate of righteousness." The first piece of weaponry is *the belt of truth*, which is God's Word. It is listed first for a reason. All the other pieces of armor are connected with the Word. If you eliminate the Word from your life, you eliminate all the remaining pieces of weaponry. The *breastplate of righteousness* is the second piece of armor mentioned. Holding onto your righteousness protects your vital organs, including the emotions of your heart.

In verse 15, Paul said, "And your feet shod with the preparation of the gospel of peace." Thus the third piece of weaponry is *shoes of peace*, which could also be called "killer shoes." They symbolically reflect the shoes worn by Roman soldiers, which had spikes attached to the soles and sharp hobnails extending from the front and back of the shoes. If anything or anyone got in the way of a soldier, they were instructed to crush them under their feet and keep on marching.

Paul added the fourth piece of armor in verse 16, saying, "Above all, taking the shield of faith, wherewith ye shall be able to quench all the fiery darts of the wicked." The soldier's shield was about the size of a door and constructed of multiple layers of leather. Before each battle, soldiers were to soak their shield in water. The saturated shield would not catch fire when the enemy troops shot fiery darts at them. Similarly, your *shield of faith* will not burn up when you enter into battle if you regularly soak it in the water of the Word (*see* Ephesians 5:26).

Furthermore, the Bible instructs us to "take the helmet of salvation, and the sword of the Spirit, which is the word of God" (Ephesians 6:17). Here we see the fifth and sixth pieces of our weaponry — the *helmet of salvation*, which is symbolic of knowing all that is yours through salvation in Christ, and the *sword of the Spirit*, which in the Greek indicates very specific scriptures that act as a double-edged dagger with which you can lethally stab the enemy.

The final piece of weaponry is the *lance of prayer*. In Ephesians 6:18, Paul said, "Praying always with all prayer and supplication in the Spirit...." Prayer enables you to do battle with the enemy and land him a damaging blow from a distance.

Your Weapons Are 'Mighty Through God'

Turning our attention once more to our anchor verse, it says, "For the weapons of our warfare are not carnal, but mighty through God to the pulling down of strong holds" (1 Corinthians 10:4). We've already seen the meaning of the word "weapons." Now let's look at the word "warfare." It is the Greek word *strateia*, which describes *a well-planned attack*. It is derived from the word *strateuomai*, which depicts *strategic warfare*. It includes *the methods to be used in an attack* and *the route chosen to carry out a debilitating assault*. This lets us know that in addition to equipping us with spiritual weapons, God will also give us a *divine strategy* to defeat the devil. If we will listen, the Holy Spirit will show us what to do.

Another important word in this verse is the word "carnal," which is the Greek word *sarkikos*. In this case it means *not fleshly, not natural; it is not derived from the fleshly, natural, or material world*. On the contrary, the weapons of our warfare are *spiritual* and they are "mighty through God." The word "mighty" is a translation of the Greek word *dunamis*, which describes *power*. It pictures *explosive, superhuman power that comes with enormous energy and produces phenomenal, extraordinary, and unparalleled results*. The word *dunamis* was used to depict *the full might and power of an advancing army*. This means when God releases His power in you, you become the aggressor.

As you advance against the enemy, the Bible says your weapons are mighty "through God." This phrase in Greek is *to Theo*, which means *through God; through the instrumentality of God; through a partnership with God*. He joins His "super" with your "natural," and together you begin "pulling down strongholds." The words "pulling down" is the Greek word *kathaireo*, which means *to take down* or *to disassemble, if needed, bit by bit*. It can also be translated *to demolish; to destroy;* or *to dismantle*. It carries such power it means *to throw down; to knock down, break up, pull apart, and take to pieces until nothing is left standing*. This word is used to picture pulling down the walls of a well-defended fortress.

This brings us back to the word "strongholds," the Greek word *ochuroma*, which describes *a fortress, a castle,* or a *citadel*. It pictures *a stronghold with walls fortified to keep outsiders on the outside*. It is also depicts *a prison* in which a person is held captive behind imaginary bars. Spiritually speaking, if a person has a stronghold, they are insulated by some kind of mental or emotional lie acting as a walled fortress in their soul. Only the supernatural weaponry offered by God can effectively demolish such places of imprisonment.

In our next lesson, we will discover the difference between logical and illogical strongholds and what is meant by "...casting down imaginations and every high thing that exalteth itself against the knowledge of God" (2 Corinthians 10:5).

STUDY QUESTIONS

Study to shew thyself approved unto God, a workman that needeth not to be ashamed, rightly dividing the word of truth.
— 2 Timothy 2:15

1. Your mind is *the control center* of your life, and Jesus wants to be Lord of it. What do Romans 12:2 and Ephesians 4:22-24 say you need to do in order for Jesus to be Lord of your mind? How do you think God's instructions in Colossians 3:1-3; Isaiah 26:3; and Philippians 4:8 relate to this? What practical steps can you take to involve yourself in this highly effective spiritual practice?

2. Carefully reread the meaning of the Greek word *diabolos* — the word translated as "devil." What new insights about the devil's mode of operation is the Holy Spirit showing you? In what ways (and in what areas) is Satan living up to this name in your life?

PRACTICAL APPLICATION

But be ye doers of the word, and not hearers only, deceiving your own selves.
—James 1:22

1. Are there areas in your mind and emotions that are currently being influenced or controlled by the enemy's lies? (Think about areas where you are experiencing fear, doubt, and worry.) In what areas do you find yourself repeatedly being attacked? Do you feel like a prisoner to these areas of your mind and emotions?

2. Carefully read Ephesians 6:14-18 and identify the seven pieces of spiritual weaponry God has given you with which to defeat the enemy. What do you think it means to "put on" your armor? Would you say you wear your armor *sporadically* or *daily*? What else is the Holy Spirit speaking to you in these verses?

3. In addition to equipping you with spiritual weapons, God will also give you a *divine strategy* to defeat the devil. In what area of your life right now do you desperately need God's divine strategy to conquer the enemy? Take a moment and pray, *"Holy Spirit, please show me the specific action I need to take to carry out a debilitating assault against Satan, in Jesus' Name."* Be still and listen. What is God speaking to you?

TOPIC

Logical and Illogical Strongholds

SCRIPTURES

1. **2 Corinthians 10:4, 5** — For the weapons of our warfare are not carnal, but mighty through God to the pulling down of strong holds. Casting down imaginations, and every high thing that exalteth itself against the knowledge of God...

GREEK WORDS

1. "warfare" — **στρατεία** (*strateia*): a well-planned attack; derived from **στρατεύομαι** (*strateuomai*), which depicts strategic warfare; methods to be used in an attack and the route chosen to carry out a debilitating assault

2. "carnal" — **σαρκικός** (*sarkikos*): fleshly; natural; whatever is derived from the fleshly, natural, or material world

3. "mighty" — **δυνατὰ** (*dunata*): from **δύναμις** (*dunamis*), power; pictures explosive, superhuman power that comes with enormous energy and produces phenomenal, extraordinary, and unparalleled results; used to depict the full might and power of an advancing army

4. "through God" — **τῷ Θεῷ** (*to Theo*): through God; through the instrumentality of God; through a partnership with God

5. "pulling down" — **καθαιρέω** (*kathaireo*): to take down; to disassemble, if needed, bit by bit; to demolish; to destroy; to dismantle; to throw down; to knock down, break up, pull apart, and take to pieces until

nothing is left standing; used to picture pulling down the walls of a well-defended fortress

6. "strongholds"— ὀχύρωμα (*ochuroma*): fortress; castle; citadel; pictures a stronghold with walls fortified to keep outsiders on the outside; a dreadful prison constructed deep inside a fortress that was intended to prevent a hostage or prisoner from escaping; a place of arrest, captivity, confinement, detention, imprisonment, or incarceration

7. "casting down"— καθαιρέω (*kathaireo*): to take down; to disassemble, if needed, bit by bit; to demolish; to destroy; to dismantle; to throw down; to knock down, break up, pull apart, and take to pieces until nothing is left standing; used to picture pulling down the walls of a well-defended fortress

8. "imaginations"— λογισμός (*logismos*): where we get the word logic, as in logical thinking; used to denote thoughts or reasoning in the mind

9. "every"— πᾶν (*pan*): all; an all-encompassing word, nothing excluded

10. "high thing"— ὕψωμα (*hupsoma*): barrier; bulwark; presumption

11. "exalted itself"— ἐπαίρω (*epairo*): to lift up; depicts a haughty, arrogant, prideful rising; to wrongfully assert

12. "against the knowledge of God"— κατὰ τῆς γνώσεως τοῦ Θεοῦ (*kata tes gnoseos tou Theou*): the word κατά (*kata*) means against; in this phrase, it means to dominate, quash, pull under its control, or to subdue; the words τῆς γνώσεως τοῦ Θεοῦ (*tes gnoseos tou Theou*) depicts knowledge that finds its origin in God or absolutely clear knowledge that comes from God; hence, this phrase depicts a war against all knowledge that comes from God

SYNOPSIS

Ivan the Terrible was a tyrant who ruled the land of Russia in the 16th Century. He began his reign at a very young age, and for that reason, his mother became his regent until he was an adult. During that time, she issued orders for a massive wall to be erected around the historic Kitay-gorod section of Moscow. It was designed with fourteen watchtowers and multiple openings within its walls where cannons and muskets were positioned to fight off invaders. And so it was between the years 1535 and 1538, this immense stronghold was built to keep out those who didn't belong and keep in those who lived inside.

This is an excellent illustration of what Second Corinthians 10:4 refers to as "stronghold." In a spiritual sense, there are people today living their lives with impregnable walls or fortresses in their souls. They are trapped as prisoners by their own vain imaginations. Thankfully, anyone that is incarcerated by the enemy's lies can break free — including you. God has given you mighty spiritual weapons to pull down any stronghold holding you hostage.

The emphasis of this lesson:

There are two main types of strongholds — logical and illogical. But regardless of the type, the effects are the same: Both are a place of enslavement that incarcerates its victim. God wants you to be free of all strongholds.

A Brief Review of Our Anchor Verse

In our previous lesson, we identified seven major weapons God has given us with which to stand against the enemy. They are found in Ephesians 6:14-18 and include *the belt of truth, the breastplate of righteousness, the shield of faith, the shoes of peace, the helmet of salvation, the sword of the Spirit,* and *the lance of prayer.*

In Second Corinthians 10:4, our anchor verse, the apostle Paul said, "… The weapons of our warfare are not carnal, but mighty through God to the pulling down of strong holds." There are several important words in this verse we need to review so that we can know and understand them.

First is the word **"warfare."** It is the Greek word *strateia*, and it describes *a well-planned attack.* It is derived from the word *strateuomai*, which depicts *strategic warfare.* This lets us know God desires and is ready to provide a strategic plan of attack for you to defeat the enemy's lies. Not only will He give you the methods, but also the best route to carry out a debilitating assault. This is a Holy-Spirit inspired strategy on how to assault the lies that are dominating your life.

The Bible says the weapons God has provided are not **"carnal,"** which means they are *not fleshly or natural* — they are *spiritual.* It also says they are **"mighty,"** which is a translation of the Greek word *dunamis*, meaning *power.* It pictures *explosive, superhuman power that comes with enormous energy and produces phenomenal, extraordinary, and unparalleled results.* This word was used to depict *the full might and power of an advancing army.* This means the Holy Spirit living inside of you not only provides you with a supernatural arsenal of artillery, but also a divine strategy to put the devil on the run.

Please note that the weapons are mighty **"through God,"** which in Greek is the phrase *to Theo*, meaning *through God; through the instrumentality of God; through a partnership with God.* Therefore, the explosive, superhuman power that comes with enormous energy and produces phenomenal, extraordinary, and unparalleled results will only manifest as we abide in relationship with God. It is the power (*dunamis*) of His Holy Spirit that enables us in the "pulling down" of strongholds.

We've seen that the phrase **"pulling down"** is the Greek word *kathaireo*, which means *to take down, throw down*, or *to disassemble, if needed, bit by bit.* This is the action God is calling you to take. He will infuse you with power *to demolish, to destroy*, and *to dismantle* the devil's fortress of deception. That is what the word *kathaireo* — translated here as "pulling down" — means. It carries such force it means *to knock down, break up, pull apart, and take to pieces until nothing is left standing.* Realize if a certain lie has been working in your mind and emotions for a long time, it may not come down quickly. Nevertheless, if you will stay committed to the Lord and the process of "pulling down" the stronghold, you will succeed.

The word **"strongholds"** is the Greek word *ochuroma*, which describes *a fortress, a castle,* or *a citadel.* It pictures *a stronghold with walls fortified to keep outsiders on the outside.* It also depicts *a dreadful prison constructed deep inside a fortress that was intended to prevent a hostage or prisoner from escaping.* Thus, a "stronghold" (*ochuroma*) is *a place of arrest, captivity, confinement, detention, imprisonment,* or *incarceration.* If you are dealing with a stronghold in your life, you will feel confined and imprisoned in that area. It will keep you moving forward in what God has for you.

The Difference Between 'Logical' and 'Illogical' Strongholds

The apostle Paul went on to say that our job as believers includes, "Casting down imaginations, and every high thing that exalteth itself against the knowledge of God…" (2 Corinthians 10:5). Interestingly, the phrase "casting down" is actually the same word for "pulling down" — the Greek word *kathaireo.* Again, it means *to take down, to throw down*, or *to disassemble, if needed, bit by bit.* It can be translated *to demolish; to destroy, to dismantle;*

to knock down, break up, pull apart, and take to pieces until nothing is left standing. It is used to picture pulling down the walls of a well-defended fortress

Specifically, Paul said we are to cast down "imaginations," which is the Greek word *logismos*. It is from where we get the word *logic*, as in *logical thinking*. It is used to denote *thoughts* or *reasoning in the mind*, and therefore identifies where the enemy's attack is taking place — in our imaginations. To be clear, a "stronghold" is anything that arrests you, confines you, or incarcerates you and keeps you from moving forward. A stronghold can be *logical* or *illogical*.

A *logical* stronghold is one that makes sense to your mind. Here is an example: God tells you to do something — maybe it is to begin a certain ministry, start a new business, or go back to school. In this case, a logical stronghold would be a lie that thinks, *God, I hear what You're saying, but I cannot do what You're telling me to do because it's not logical.* A logical stronghold will arrest you and keep you from taking a step of faith. This kind is very difficult to deal with because it is logical. The bottom line is, if God gives us a word of instruction, we need to do what He says — period. His word overrides our logic. If you find yourself not stepping out in obedience to do what God tells you to do, you are bound by a logical stronghold.

Then there are *illogical* strongholds, which have to do with unrealistic worries and fears. An example of this would be a skinny person who consistently looks into the mirror and sees himself as fat. What they see about themselves does *not* match reality, but it is real to them. They are concerned that if they eat, they are going to get into trouble physically. Therefore, they starve themselves and become anorexic. That is totally illogical. The truth is they're too skinny, and their health is in jeopardy. If they don't start eating, it's going to drastically affect their well-being. This is an example of an *illogical* stronghold. Yet, whether a stronghold is logical or illogical, its effects are just the same. Both are a place of arrest that incarcerates its victim.

Cast Down Anything That 'Exalts Itself Against the Knowledge of God'

In addition to casting down imaginations, Paul instructs us to cast down "...every high thing that exalteth itself against the knowledge of God..."

(2 Corinthians 10:5). First of all, the word "every" is the Greek word *pan*, and it is *an all-encompassing word*, indicating *all, nothing excluded*. The words "high thing" is a translation of the Greek word *hupsoma*, which describes *a barrier, a bulwark*; or *a presumption*. Thus, anything that is blocking you from stepping forward in faith to do what you know God has asked you to do He wants you to cast down.

The Bible describes these barriers or presumptions as something that "… exalted itself against the knowledge of God…." The phrase "exalteth itself" is the Greek word *epairo*, which means *to lift up*. It depicts *a haughty, arrogant, prideful rising*; it can also mean *to wrongfully assert*. This haughty, prideful attitude rises up "against the knowledge of God." In the Greek, this phrase is *kata tes gnoseos tou Theou*. The word *kata* means *against*, and in this phrase, it means *to dominate, quash, pull under its control*, or *to subdue*. The words *tes gnoseos tou Theou* depict *knowledge that finds its origin in God* or *absolutely clear knowledge that comes from God*. Hence, this phrase depicts *a war against all knowledge that comes from God*. Here is an example.

The Bible says by Jesus' "…stripes ye are healed" (1 Peter 2:24). That is knowledge that comes from God. There are people who have a stronghold in their mind that says, *Well I know the Bible says we're healed by Jesus' stripes, but the reality is, I'm not healed. And I've been trying to be healed for a long time. I'll probably never be healed.* Did you catch that? The lie in the minds of these people exalts itself against the knowledge of God.

Or how about this: God says in His Word that you are *the righteousness of God in Christ Jesus* (*see* 2 Corinthians 5:21). That is clear knowledge that comes from God. However, you may have a stronghold that fights against this truth. Thoughts and feelings of unworthiness in your mind lie to you, bringing condemnation, guilt, and a sense of unrighteousness. This is what the Bible calls a "high thing" — a barrier or presumption — that arrogantly "exalteth itself" and wars against the knowledge of God. It is a stronghold fighting against what God says about you.

Friend, if there's anything that is squashing the truth of God's Word — anything contrary to what Scripture says that is trying to take you down, control you, or dominate you —it is a stronghold and does not belong in your thinking. You need to grab hold of the mighty weapons God has given you and aggressively pull it down, dismantle it, disassemble it, or take it apart bit-by-bit if needed until no trace of it remains operating in you.

STUDY QUESTIONS

Study to shew thyself approved unto God, a workman that
needeth not to be ashamed, rightly dividing the word of truth.
— 2 Timothy 2:15

1. A "stronghold" is anything that arrests you, confines you, or incarcerates you and keeps you from moving forward in faith. It can be *logical* or *illogical*. In your own words, explain the difference between these two. What is the bottom line when it comes to God speaking a word of direction to you?

2. Many believers battle strongholds of *worry, fear*, and *condemnation*. Take time to slowly soak in these promises from God once a day for the next seven days (consider reading them in several different Bible versions). When you complete the week of reflection, journal any changes you experience in your thinking as well as your level of trust in God.

   No Worry: Matthew 6:25-34; Luke 12:22-34; Philippians 4:6-8

   No Fear: Isaiah 41:10-14; Hebrews 13:5,6; Psalm 121; Proverbs 3:24-26

   No Condemnation: John 3:16-18; Romans 8:1,2,31,33,34; 1 John 3:19-21

PRACTICAL APPLICATION

But be ye doers of the word, and not hearers only,
deceiving your own selves.
— James 1:22

1. Give at least one example of a *logical* and an *illogical* stronghold that the devil has tried to establish in your life (either past or present). Which was more difficult to deal with? Why?

2. First Corinthians 12:7 says, "Each person is given something to do that shows who God is." To the best of your understanding, what assignment has God given you in your current season of life? (It may be more than one.) Are you doing it? If not, what stronghold of thinking is the enemy using to block you from stepping out in faith to do it?

3. What steps can you start taking now to cast down these imaginations and lies of begin to obey God and move forward in doing His plan?

TOPIC

Bringing Every Thought Into Captivity

SCRIPTURES

1. **2 Corinthians 10:4,5** — For the weapons of our warfare are not carnal, but mighty through God to the pulling down of strong holds. Casting down imaginations, and every high thing that exalteth itself against the knowledge of God, and bringing into captivity every thought to the obedience of Christ.

2. **Ephesians 6:14-18** — Stand therefore, having your loins girt about with truth, and having on the breastplate of righteousness; and your feet shod with the preparation of the gospel of peace. Above all, taking the shield of faith, wherewith ye shall be able to quench all the fiery darts of the wicked. And take the helmet of salvation, and the sword of the Spirit, which is the word of God. Praying always with all prayer and supplication in the Spirit..."

3. **1 Samuel 17:38-40** — And Saul armed David with his armour, and he put an helmet of brass upon his head; also he armed him with a coat of mail. And David girded his sword upon his armour, and he assayed to go; for he had not proved it. And David said unto Saul, I cannot go with these; for I have not proved them. And David put them off him. And he took his staff in his hand, and chose him five smooth stones out of the brook, and put them in a shepherd's bag which he had, even in a scrip; and his sling was in his hand: and he drew near to the Philistine.

4. **Romans 10:17** — So then faith cometh by hearing and hearing....

GREEK WORDS

1. "weapons" — ὅπλα (*hopla*): from ὅπλον (*hoplon*), armor, weapons; used in Ephesians 6:14-18 to depict the whole armor of God that potentially belongs to every believer

2. "warfare" — **στρατεία** (*strateia*): a well-planned attack; derived from **στρατεύομαι** (*strateuomai*), which depicts strategic warfare; methods to be used in an attack and the route chosen to carry out a debilitating assault

3. "carnal" — **σαρκικός** (*sarkikos*): fleshly; natural; whatever is derived from the fleshly, natural, or material world

4. "mighty" — **δυνατὰ** (*dunata*): from **δύναμις** (*dunamis*), power; pictures explosive, superhuman power that comes with enormous energy and produces phenomenal, extraordinary, and unparalleled results; used to depict the full might and power of an advancing army

5. "through God" — **τῷ Θεῷ** (*to Theo*): through God; through the instrumentality of God; through a partnership with God

6. "pulling down" — **καθαιρέω** (*kathaireo*): to take down; to disassemble, if needed, bit by bit; to demolish; to destroy; to dismantle; to throw down; to knock down, break up, pull apart, and take to pieces until nothing is left standing; used to picture pulling down the walls of a well-defended fortress

7. "strongholds" — **ὀχύρωμα** (*ochuroma*): fortress; castle; citadel; pictures a stronghold with walls fortified to keep outsiders on the outside; a dreadful prison constructed deep inside a fortress that was intended to prevent a hostage or prisoner from escaping; a place of arrest, captivity, confinement, detention, imprisonment, or incarceration

8. "casting down" — **καθαιρέω** (*kathaireo*): to take down; to disassemble, if needed, bit by bit; to demolish; to destroy; to dismantle; to throw down; to knock down, break up, pull apart, and take to pieces until nothing is left standing; used to picture pulling down the walls of a well-defended fortress

9. "imaginations" — **λογισμός** (*logismos*): where we get the word logic, as in logical thinking; used to denote thoughts or reasoning in the mind

10. "every" — **πᾶν** (*pan*): all; an all-encompassing word, nothing excluded

11. "high thing" — **ὕψωμα** (*hupsoma*): barrier; bulwark; presumption

12. "exalted itself" — **ἐπαίρω** (*epairo*): to lift up; depicts a haughty, arrogant, prideful rising; to wrongfully assert

13. "against the knowledge of God" — **κατὰ τῆς γνώσεως τοῦ Θεοῦ** (*kata tes gnoseos tou Theou*): the word **κατά** (*kata*) means against; in this phrase, it means to dominate, quash, pull under its control, or to subdue; the words **τῆς γνώσεως τοῦ Θεοῦ** (*tes gnoseos tou Theou*) depicts knowledge that finds its origin in God or absolutely clear knowledge

that comes from God; hence, this phrase depicts a war against all knowledge that comes from God

14. "bringing into captivity" — αἰχμαλωτίζω (*aichmalotidzo*): pictures a soldier who has captured an enemy and leads him into captivity with the point of a sharpened spear thrust into his back; the captive doesn't dare resist, but is silent, submissive, and non-resistant; to force one into obedience, submission, and slavery; to bring under control; to lead into captivity

15. "thought" — νόημα (*noema*): thought; insinuation; includes emotions

16. "obedience" — ὑπακούω (*hupakouo*): from ὑπό (*hupo*) and ακούω (*akouo*); the word ὑπό (*hupo*) means under and implies a subservient position; the word ακούω (*akouo*) means to listen: pictures one who listens willingly or by force and who obeys what he hears either willing or by pressure

17. "Christ" — χριστός (*Christos*): Christ, the One who is anointed; the anointing

SYNOPSIS

In our previous lessons, we have talked about the ancient walls of the Kitay-gorod. These massive barriers were as thick as they were wide, and they were erected between the years of 1535 and 1538 at the order of Ivan the Terrible's mother. The purpose for building this fortification was to protect the affluent residents living in the region from outside invaders. Unfortunately, the same walls that provided protected also trapped those living within the walls. This is a perfect example of a *stronghold* and how it operates. And just as there are strongholds in the natural realm, there are also strongholds in the spiritual realm. In the natural realm, the walls are made of brick and mortar; in the spiritual realm, the walls are made of lies that come in the form of thoughts and feelings.

The emphasis of this lesson:

In order to pull down strongholds in your life, you must cast down imaginations and every thought in your mind that arrogantly rises up in defiance of the Word of God.

You Have Been Given Mighty Spiritual Weapons

The apostle Paul wrote about strongholds in Second Corinthians 10:4, which says, "For the weapons of our warfare are not carnal, but mighty through God to the pulling down of strong holds." We have seen that the word "weapons" is the Greek word *hopla*, from the word *hoplon*, which describes *armor* or *weapons*. It is the same root word Paul used in Ephesians 6:11 when he instructed us to "Put on the whole *armour* of God, that ye may be able to stand against the wiles of the devil."

In the same chapter, just a few verses later, we are given a list of seven specific weapons with which we are to dress ourselves and use in our spiritual fight. Paul said, "Stand therefore, having your loins girt about with truth, and having on the breastplate of righteousness; and your feet shod with the preparation of the gospel of peace" (Ephesians 6:14, 15).

In these two verses, we see three pieces of weaponry: *the loinbelt of truth, the breastplate of righteousness,* and *the shoes of peace.* What's interesting is that when you understand that the shoes of a Roman soldier were covered with sharp, protruding nails in the front, back, and underneath, *killer shoes* would be a better name for them. Spiritually speaking, when you walk in your *shoes of peace,* you have the ability to crush the enemy under your feet! (*See* Romans 16:20.)

The Bible goes on to say, "Above all, taking the shield of faith, wherewith ye shall be able to quench all the fiery darts of the wicked" (Ephesians 6:16). In Greek, this verse doesn't say "above all." It actually says, *"Out in front of all."* Thus, *the shield of faith* is not more important than the other weapons; it is supposed to be out in front of them. "Above all" describes the *position* of our faith. When you use your faith correctly and put it out in front of everything else, you will "…be able to quench all the fiery darts of the wicked."

Two more weapons are found in Ephesians 6:17: "…*the helmet of salvation,* and *the sword of the Spirit,* which is the word of God." When the Scripture talks about the helmet of salvation, it is talking about having your thoughts protected by knowing all that is yours through salvation in Jesus Christ. The final piece of weaponry is listed in Ephesians 6:18, which says, "Praying always with all prayer and supplication in the Spirit…." The *lance of intercession* is the weapon we see here.

These seven weapons make up the *panoplia* — or the "whole armor" — of God. This lets us know that God has left nothing out or held anything back. He has given us everything we need to make sure we are covered from head to toe, side to side, front to back.

David Demonstrated God's Divine Empowerment

There is an amazing story found in First Samuel 17 about a young shepherd boy named David who demonstrated the supernatural use of weaponry. He had been sent to the battlefront by his father Jesse to check on his brothers and see how things were going. Shortly after he arrived, he heard the blasphemous torments of Goliath, the giant from Gath, and was outraged by his insolence. Immediately, he decided he would go out and defeat the uncircumcised Philistine.

When David voiced his intentions to King Saul, the Bible says, "And Saul armed David with his armour, and he put an helmet of brass upon his head; also he armed him with a coat of mail. And David girded his sword upon his armour, and he assayed to go; for he had not proved it..." (1 Samuel 17:38, 39). After the king dressed David in his armor, David tested it out and quickly concluded, "...I cannot go with these; for I have not proved them. And David put them off him" (vs. 39).

The Scripture goes on the say, "And he [David] took his staff in his hand, and chose him five smooth stones out of the brook, and put them in a shepherd's bag which he had, even in a scrip; and his sling was in his hand: and he drew near to the Philistine" (1 Samuel 17:40).

In this verse we see that David had weapons: a sling, some stones, and a shepherd's bag in which to hold them. These weapons were not mighty in the natural, but they became mighty through God to "pull down" Goliath. In the mind of Israel, the giant was a "stronghold" spouting lies that imprisoned the nation in fear. David trusted in the name of the Lord and His faithfulness and effectively used his weapons to destroy the enemy (*see* 1 Samuel 17:50).

Along With Weapons, God Supplies Divine *Strategy* and *Power*

Looking once more at our anchor verse, it says, "For the weapons of our warfare are not carnal, but mighty through God to the pulling down of strong holds" (2 Corinthians 10:4). We have noted that the word "warfare" is the Greek word *strateia*, and it describes *a well-planned attack*. It is derived from the word *strateuomai*, which depicts *strategic warfare*. So in addition to God giving us weaponry, this word indicates that He will also give us *divine strategy* on how to use our weapons — and tell us the best route to choose to carry out a debilitating assault against our enemy.

To be clear, you are equipped to wage a debilitating assault against anything that comes against you. Moreover, the weapons you have are not "carnal," which is the Greek word *sarkikos*, meaning *fleshly* or *natural*. In the context here, Paul is telling us there is nothing fleshly or natural about our weapons. They are *spiritual* weapons with which to win a spiritual fight.

Furthermore, the weapons you have been given are "mighty." This is the Greek word *dunata*, which is from the word *dunamis*, meaning *power*. It pictures *explosive, superhuman power that comes with enormous energy and produces phenomenal, extraordinary, and unparalleled results*. It is the word used to depict *the full might and power of an advancing army*. This means, when you have the mighty power of God (*dunamis*) and His divine strategy, you are in a position to advance and deliver a debilitating assault to defeat the enemy.

It is also important to note that the weapons you have are mighty "through God." The words "through God" in Greek is *to Theo*, which means *through God; through the instrumentality of God; through a partnership with God*. This signifies that when you decide in your heart to advance and defeat the enemy, God joins Himself to you by His Spirit, enabling you to "pull down" the strongholds in your life.

The phrase "pulling down" is the Greek word *kathaireo*, which means *to take down, to throw down*, or *to disassemble, if needed, bit by bit*. In can also be translated *to demolish; to destroy; to dismantle*; or *to knock down, break up, pull apart, and take to pieces, until nothing is left standing*. To effectively "pull down" the enemy's strongholds, we have to be totally committed to attack and tear them to pieces until nothing remains.

Cast Down Imaginations and All Ungodly Thinking

The apostle Paul clarified that tearing down strongholds requires, "Casting down imaginations, and every high thing that exalteth itself against the knowledge of God…" (2 Corinthians 10:5). We saw that the phrase "casting down" is the Greek word *kathaireo*, which is the exact same word translated as "pulling down" in verse 4. Again, it means *to take down, to knock down, to destroy,* or *to dismantle, if needed, bit by bit until nothing is left standing.*

What are we *breaking apart* and *tearing to pieces*? First, Paul said "imaginations," which is the Greek word *logismos*. It is from where we get the word *logic*, as in *logical thinking*, and it denotes *reasonings in the mind*. A stronghold is a well-established and well-defended *fortress of lies* located in the area of the mind. Little by little — one deceptive thought at a time — we accept and give place to Satan's lies until a stronghold is established. He then moves in and begins to rule over areas of our life. Like a tyrant, he begins to tell us what to think, how we feel, who we are, and what we are not. The Bible classifies these things as "imaginations."

Additionally, Paul said we are to cast down "...every high thing that exalteth itself against the knowledge of God..." (2 Corinthians 10:5). We saw in a previous lesson that the word "every" is the Greek word *pan*, which describes *something that is all-encompassing, nothing excluded*. And the phrase "high thing" is the Greek word *hupsoma*, which depicts *a barrier, a bulwark,* or *a presumption*. Wrong thoughts and beliefs act as a wall that "exalteth itself against the knowledge of God."

The phrase "exalteth itself" in Greek is the word *epairo*, which means *to lift up* or *to wrongfully assert*. It depicts *a haughty, arrogant, prideful rising*; it is a prideful way of thinking that wrongfully stands up "against the knowledge of God." In Greek, "against the knowledge of God" is *kata tes gnoseos rou theou*. The word *kata* means *against*, and in this phrase, it means *to dominate, quash, pull under its control,* or *to subdue*. The words *tes gnoseos rou theou*, depict *knowledge that finds its origin in God* or *absolutely clear knowledge that comes from God*. Hence, this phrase depicts *a war against all knowledge that comes from God*.

The truth is, there are voices speaking to you all the time. These may include your parents, your teachers, your spouse, and your friends — not to mention the voice of the media, politicians, and your pastor. These voices are talking to you all the time, and you have to be careful about what voices you listen to. Of all the voices you hear, two are usually louder than all the rest. They are the voice of God and the voice of the enemy. Both of them want your mind, because your mind is the control central of your life. Whoever dominates your mind will build a stronghold there, and from that stronghold they will begin to dominate and direct your thoughts, your emotions, your self-image, and your entire life. The one who controls your mind controls you.

Make no mistake: God speaks the truth, the whole truth, and nothing but the truth. The devil speaks lies because he is the father of lies and that is all he knows how to speak (*see* John 8:44). For example, God says, you are the righteousness of God in Christ and made acceptable in Him (*see* 2 Corinthians 5:21; Ephesians 1:6). That is knowledge that originates and comes from God. The voice of the enemy says, "You're not righteous. You don't behave righteous. In fact, you should be ashamed of yourself." Again and again, the devil (*diabolos*) strikes your mind and emotions with thoughts and feelings of condemnation, guilt, and worthlessness. In those moments, the voice you choose to listen to, believe, and act on will determine what you experience.

"Casting down imaginations and every high thing that exalteth itself against the knowledge of God" is rejecting the enemy's lies and believing the truth of God's Word. Whatever God says about you in His Word is the truth. And Jesus said if you continue in His Word, "Ye shall know the truth, and the truth shall make you free" (John 8:32).

Bring Into Captivity Every Thought to the Obedience of Christ

The second part of Second Corinthians 10:5 says, "…bringing into captivity every thought to the obedience of Christ." The phrase "bringing into captivity" in Greek is the word *aichmalotidzo*, which pictures *a soldier who has captured an enemy and leads him into captivity with the point of a sharpened spear thrust into his back*; the captive doesn't dare resist, but is silent, submissive, and non-resistant. This word can also mean *to force one into obedience, submission, and slavery*; *to bring under control*; or *to lead into captivity*.

The use of this word tells us that when wrong thoughts come against our mind, we need to take the sharpened sword of the Spirit (God's Word) and thrust it against the enemy. That is, you need to open your mouth and say to the thoughts — and the spirit behind the thoughts — "You are not going to dictate what I think and believe. You are now bound by the authority of Jesus Christ, and I take you captive by the eternal truth of His Word" (*see* Matthew 16:19; Luke 10:19).

The Bible says we are to bring into captivity "…every thought to the obedience of Christ." In Greek, the word "every" is again the word *pan*, which indicates *something all-encompassing, nothing excluded*. And the word "thought" is the Greek word *noema*, which describes *a thought* or *an insinuation; it includes emotions*. Every single thought that does not agree and line up with the truth of the Word must be brought to the "obedience of Christ."

The word "obedience" is the Greek word *hupakouo*. It is from the word *hupo*, meaning *under* and implies *a subservient position*; and the word *akouo*, meaning *to listen*. When these words are compounded, the word *hupakouo* pictures *one who listens willingly or by force and who obeys what he hears either willing or by pressure*. This indicates that when wrong, ungodly thoughts come against your mind, you are to say to them, "You are going to listen and submit to the truth of God's Word whether you like it or not. You are not going to dictate to what I am going to think or how I am going to feel anymore. I'm taking you to Christ, and you are going to obey Him!"

The word "Christ" is the Greek word *christos*, which means *Christ, One Who is Anointed*. It is also the word for *the anointing*. It is the anointing of Jesus Christ and the anointing on His Word operating in your life that destroys the burdensome lies that are keeping you in bondage (*see* Isaiah 10:27). Friend, it is time to make a decision to stop listening to the lies of the enemy and start listening to the truth of God's Word. As you keep on listening and listening and listening to the truth, it will become embedded in your brain, and you will be empowered to speak to the lies and bring them captive under the authority of Jesus Christ!

STUDY QUESTIONS

> **Study to shew thyself approved unto God, a workman that needeth not to be ashamed, rightly dividing the word of truth.**
> **— 2 Timothy 2:15**

1. Do you wonder if you can hear God's voice? If so, you don't have to wonder anymore. You can! According to these promises from God's Word, what can you know for sure about the voice of God? See John 10:4, 5, 27; 16:12, 13; Psalm 32:8; Isaiah 30:21, 30; and Revelation 3:20.

2. The two loudest voices that speak to you are that of God and the enemy. What's interesting is that both will speak to you through other people and other means. How do you know when the Spirit of God is speaking to you and when the enemy is speaking to you? What is the difference in their voice prints?

PRACTICAL APPLICATION

**But be ye doers of the word, and not hearers only,
deceiving your own selves.
—James 1:22**

1. What are the most successful methods you have learned to use to silence the devil's voice when he is roaring inside your head?
2. When you feel heavily assaulted in your mind and emotions, who do you know you can turn to for prayer and support? If you don't have someone, prayerfully begin to look for a friend with whom you can talk and pray and who will help you break free from the enemy's lies.

LESSON 5

TOPIC

How To Help Others Get Free From Mental Strongholds

SCRIPTURES

1. **2 Corinthians 10:4, 5** — For the weapons of our warfare are not carnal, but mighty through God to the pulling down of strong holds. Casting down imaginations, and every high thing that exalteth itself against the knowledge of God, and bringing into captivity every thought to the obedience of Christ.
2. **Isaiah 10:27** — And it shall come to pass in that day, that his burden shall be taken away from off thy shoulder, and his yoke from off thy neck, and the yoke shall be destroyed because of the anointing.

3. **Acts 10:38** — How God anointed Jesus of Nazareth with the Holy Ghost and with power: who went about doing good, and healing all that were oppressed of the devil; for God was with him.

4. **1 John 3:8** — ...For this purpose the Son of God was manifested, that he might destroy the works of the devil.

5. **Luke 3:16** — ... one mightier than I cometh, the latchet of whose shoes I am not worthy to unloose: he shall baptize you with the Holy Ghost and with fire.

6. **1 John 2:20** — But ye have an unction from the Holy One....

GREEK WORDS

1. "casting down"— **καθαιρέω** (*kathaireo*): to take down; to disassemble, if needed, bit by bit; to demolish; to destroy; to dismantle; to throw down; to knock down, break up, pull apart, and take to pieces until nothing is left standing; used to picture pulling down the walls of a well-defended fortress

2. "imaginations"— **λογισμός** (*logismos*): where we get the word logic, as in logical thinking; used to denote thoughts or reasoning in the mind

3. "Christ"— **χριστός** (*Christos*): Christ, the One who is anointed; the anointing

4. "anointed"— **χρίω** (*chrio*): the rubbing of oil on an individual; used in a medical sense for "healing ointment"; scripturally used to denote the anointing of the Holy Spirit and all the effects that He brings to one who is anointed; root for the word "Christian"

5. "power"— **δύναμις** (*dunamis*): power; pictures explosive, superhuman power that comes with enormous energy and produces phenomenal, extraordinary, and unparalleled results; used to depict the full might and power of an advancing army

6. "healing"— **ἰάομαι** (*iaomai*): to cure; to be doctored; healing power that progressively reverses a condition; denotes healing that comes to pass over a period of time; for this reason, this word is often translated as a treatment, cure, or remedy; depicts a sickness that has been progressively healed rather than instantaneously healed

7. "destroy"— **λύω** (*luo*): to untie, unravel, loosen, set free, or release; same word used in Luke 3:16

8. "unloose"— **λύω** (*luo*): to untie, unravel, loosen, set free, or release

9. "oppressed" — **καταδυναστεύω** (*katadunasteuo*): a compound of **κατα** (*kata*) and **δυνάστης** (*dunastes*); the word **κατα** (*kata*) carries the idea of domination; the word **δυνάστης** (*dunastes*) depicts a dominating tyrant; when compounded, it pictures a wicked tyrant who rules over his subjects; bullying; cruelty; despotism; dictatorship; oppressiveness; tyranny

10. "devil" — **διάβολος** (*diabolos*): one who repetitiously strikes until successfully penetrating an object to ruin it, affect it, or take it captive; to slander, accuse, or defame; to penetrate by continuous assault; to ensnare with a net

11. "unction" — **χρίσμα** (*chrisma*): anointing; smeared, covered, or saturated with the anointing

SYNOPSIS

The ancient walls surrounding the Kitay-gorod section of the city of Moscow are an excellent example of what the Bible refers to as a *stronghold*. Built between the years of 1535 and 1538, these high, thick walls served to keep outsiders out and those on the inside in. A stronghold has the ability to trap and imprison a person in a fortress of lies. Not only is that person locked in, but people with the truth on the outside are locked out. Anyone — regardless of their gender, ethnicity, background, level of education, or financial condition — is vulnerable to having strongholds built in their mind. If you or someone you know is enslaved by wrong thinking, there is a way out. There are concrete steps you can take to help others break free from strongholds.

The emphasis of this lesson:

To help a person successfully break free from a stronghold, position them near the anointing of God. As they hear the Word spoken again and again and again, the anointing will demolish the devil's lies and release freedom in their lives.

How a Stronghold Works

Second Corinthians 10:4 says, "For the weapons of our warfare are not carnal, but mighty through God to the pulling down of strong holds." The word "strong holds" is the ancient Greek word *ochuroma*, which was used to describe two things. First, it described *a fortress, a castle*, or *a citadel*. It

depicted *a stronghold with thick walls fortified to keep outsiders on the outside.*
The word *ochuroma* — translated here as "stronghold" — also described *a dreadful prison constructed deep inside a fortress that was intended to prevent a hostage or prisoner from escaping.* Thus, it was *a place of arrest, captivity, confinement, detention, imprisonment, or incarceration.*

A person that has a mental stronghold has been arrested by the devil. He believes a lie, and it has put his life on pause. For example, he or she believes their marriage will never get better or that their kids are beyond hope or that their finances will never change. They may be enslaved to lies about themselves, such as they will never lose weight, they will never find someone who truly loves them, or that they are not talented or skilled enough to make a positive impact on the world around them. The list of lies a person can be ensnared by is virtually endless. Although these thoughts appear to be facts and feel very true, they are nothing but lies.

The person imprisoned by a stronghold of lies feels like they are behind bars looking out at those who are free, wishing they could be free too. When people on the outside, who see them accurately, come to them, they try to tell them that what they're thinking is not true — that their situation isn't as bad as they think and God has a good plan for their lives. But the impenetrable walls of the stronghold prevent the truth from reaching the person trapped on the inside. Little by little, one thought at a time, the devil has fed this person the same lie again and again and again, and now they believe it to be true.

Three Major Steps to Pulling Down Strongholds

'Cast Down Imaginations'

How can a person break free from a fortress of confusion and deception that dominates their life? The answer is found in Second Corinthians 10:5: "Casting down imaginations, and every high thing that exalteth itself against the knowledge of God, and bringing into captivity every thought to the obedience of Christ."

In our previous lessons, we have learned that the phrase "casting down" is the Greek word *kathaireo*, which means *to take down* or *to disassemble, if needed, bit by bit.* It can also be translated *to demolish; to destroy; to dismantle; to throw down;* or *to knock down, break up, pull apart, and take to pieces until nothing is left standing.* This is the picture of a strong commitment and great determination to utterly annihilate the enemy's well-defended fortress.

What are we to "cast down"? The Bible says "imaginations," which in Greek is the word *logismos*, and it is from where we get the word *logic*, as in *logical thinking*. It is used to denote *thoughts or reasoning in the mind*. We noted that these imaginations can be *logical* or *illogical*. *Logical* strongholds are made up of thoughts that make logical sense. *Illogical* strongholds are fortified by unrealistic worries and fears that have no basis in reality. In either case, the lie believed makes one deceived and enslaves the victim in deception.

You don't have to believe and receive every thought that falls into your head. You can take authority over them and cast them down! Use the mighty weapons God has given you (*see* Ephesians 6:14-18), and begin to cast down imaginations and "every high thing that exalteth itself against the knowledge of God..." (2 Corinthians 10:5).

'Bring Into Captivity Every Thought to the Obedience of Christ'

Next, the Bible says we are to bring "...into captivity every thought to the obedience of Christ." The phrase "bringing into captivity" in Greek is the word *aichmalotidzo*, which pictures *a soldier who has captured an enemy and leads him into captivity with the point of a sharpened spear thrust into his back*; the captive doesn't dare resist, but is silent, submissive, and non-resistant. In this case, the enemy being led into captivity is the wrong thought and the lying spirit that brought it. It is a picture of you speaking to your thoughts and directing them instead of being complacent and letting them speak and direct you.

Scripture says we are to bring into captivity "every thought." The word "every" is the word *pan*, which describes *something all-encompassing, nothing excluded*. And the word "thought" is the Greek word *noema*, which describes *a thought* or *an insinuation*. This means you are to arrest every single thought and insinuation that enters your mind that does not agree or line up with the truth of God's Word. You are to take it captive "to the obedience of Christ."

The word "obedience" is the Greek word *hupakouo*. It is from the word *hupo*, meaning *under* and carries the idea of *a subservient position*; and the word *akouo*, meaning *to listen*. When these words are compounded, the word *hupakouo* pictures *one who listens willingly or by force and who obeys what he hears either willingly or by pressure.* This indicates that when wrong, ungodly thoughts come against your mind, you are to say to them, "You are going to listen and submit to the truth of God's Word whether you like it or not! You're not going to dictate to me what to think or how to live anymore. I'm taking you to Christ, and you are going to obey Him!"

The word "Christ" is the Greek word *christos*, which means *Christ, One Who is Anointed.* It is also the root word for *the anointing.* It is the anointing of Jesus Christ and the anointing on His Word operating in your life that destroys the oppressive lies that are keeping you mentally and emotionally incarcerated.

'Saturate Your Mind in the Anointing'

There is a powerful principle about the anointing of God found in Isaiah 10:27. It says, "And it shall come to pass in that day, that his burden shall be taken away from off thy shoulder, and his yoke from off thy neck, and *the yoke shall be destroyed because of the anointing.*" The greatest key to being set free is to saturate your mind and emotions in the anointing. It is the anointing that breaks the yoke.

Acts 10:38 confirms this. It says, "How God *anointed* Jesus of Nazareth with the Holy Ghost and with power: who went about doing good, and healing all that were oppressed of the devil; for God was with him." The word "anointed" here is the Greek word *chrio*, and it describes *the rubbing of oil on an individual.* This word was used in a medical sense for "healing ointment." Scripturally, it was used to denote *the anointing of the Holy Spirit and all the effects that He brings to one who is anointed.* The word *chrio* is also the root for the word "Christian."

Jesus Christ — the firstborn among many Christian brothers and sisters — was *anointed* with the Holy Spirit and with "power." The word "power" is the Greek word *dunamis*, which depicts *explosive, superhuman power that comes with enormous energy and produces phenomenal, extraordinary, and unparalleled results.* It is the same root word translated as "mighty" in Second Corinthians 10:4, and it is used to depict *the full might and power of an advancing army.*

Clothed with the anointing of the Holy Spirit and power, Jesus "…went about doing good, and *healing* all that were oppressed of the devil…" (Acts 10:38). The word "healing" here is the Greek word *iaomai*, which is important to note. There are a number of other Greek words for healing that could have been used in this verse, but the Holy Spirit chose *iaomai*, and with good reason. *"Iaomai"* means *to cure* or *to be doctored*. It describes *healing power that progressively reverses a condition; healing that comes to pass over a period of time*. For this reason, the word *iaomai* is often translated as *a treatment, cure,* or *remedy;* it depicts *a sickness that has been progressively healed rather than instantaneously healed.*

Many times when the devil has built a stronghold in a person's mind, it takes time for the anointing of God to attack it and penetrate it with truth. The healing that takes place is *progressive (iaomai)*. Little by little, day by day, over a period of time, the anointing and power of God begins to unravel, dismantle, and disassemble that stronghold.

This principle of progressive healing is also seen in First John 3:8, which says, "...For this purpose the Son of God was manifested, that he might destroy the works of the devil." The word "destroy" here is the Greek word *luo*, which means *to untie, unravel, loosen, set free,* or *release*. It is actually the same word used in Luke 3:16 where John the Baptist said, "… one mightier than I cometh, the latchet of whose shoes I am not worthy to unloose: he shall baptize you with the Holy Ghost and with fire."

What is interesting is that the word "unloose" in Luke 3:16 is the same Greek word translated "destroy" in First John 3:8 — it is the Greek word *luo*, meaning *to untie, unravel, loosen, set free,* or *release*. What does the untying of shoes have to do with Jesus "destroying" the works of the devil? Think about how you untie your shoes and apply it to pulling down a stronghold. When you untie your shoes, you loosen one string at a time until eventually they become loose enough to take them off and free your feet. Similarly, we often have to "untie" or "loosen" the works of the devil little by little. Again, it is a progressive healing *(iaomai)* of the mind that takes place over a period of time.

Put the Principle of Faith To Work in Your Life

The Bible says, "So then faith cometh by hearing, and hearing by the word of God" (Romans 10:17). This is *the principle of faith*. It means our faith — what we believe at the core of who we are — is generated by what we hear again and again and again. In other words, faith comes by *hearing* and *hearing* and *hearing* and *hearing*. The devil understands this principle, and therefore, continues to speak his lies over and over and over again. He knows if you hear it and hear it and hear it and hear it, eventually you will begin to believe — or have faith in — the lies he speaks.

Thankfully, the opposite is also true. If you choose to close your mind to the enemy's lies and only listen to what the anointed Word of God says about you and your situations, you will be healed. If you will fill your mind with the anointed Word of God and hear the Word and hear the Word and hear the Word, eventually your mind will be filled with faith in what God says, and it will become reality in your life. What you hear determines what you become. This is true for you and any friend who may be imprisoned in a stronghold of vain imaginations.

Remember, it is the anointing that breaks the yoke! It is the anointing that sets the captives free! If you know someone being held hostage by a stronghold of lies, bring them into an environment where the anointing is being released. This includes attending a good church where they consistently hear anointed teaching. Likewise, it involves hearing anointed Christian teaching on the Internet, TV, and radio. It would also include reading the anointed Word of God and anointed books. When you inundate and saturate the mind of a person held captive by lies with the anointing of God, they will progressively receive the healing (*iaomai*) for which they look and long.

Friend, just as Jesus was anointed and went about healing all who were oppressed of the devil, you are called to do likewise. Now you may be thinking, *Well, that was Jesus. He could do that, but I can't.* But that is not true. The Bible declares in First John 2:20, "Ye have an unction from the Holy One...." The word "unction" in this verse is the Greek word *chrisma*, which describes *the anointing*. It carries the idea of being *smeared, covered, or saturated with the anointing from head to toe.*

You are a *Christian*, and the word "Christian" comes from the Greek word *chrio*, which is the root of the word "anointed." This means the same anointing that was on Jesus is now on you. The same Holy Spirit that anointed Him has also anointed you. You have been anointed with *dunamis* power — the spiritual power of an advancing army. Therefore, you are anointed to heal anyone who is oppressed by the devil, just as Jesus did. It is His power and anointing flowing through you to others. If you know anyone who is dealing with a debilitating stronghold, do what is in your power to get them near the anointing of God.

STUDY QUESTIONS

Study to shew thyself approved unto God, a workman that needeth not to be ashamed, rightly dividing the word of truth.
— 2 Timothy 2:15

1. The greatest key to being set free from the enemy's strongholds is to saturate your mind and emotions in the anointing. What new facets of God's anointing did you learn about in this lesson? How do you see yourself differently when it comes to the anointing? (Consider 1 John 2:20, 27; 2 Corinthians 1:21, 22; Romans 8:11.)

2. Acts 10:38 says, "God anointed Jesus of Nazareth with the Holy Ghost and with power: who went about doing good, and *healing* all that were oppressed of the devil...." The word for "healing" here means that Jesus went about *progressively healing* people. How does this meaning expand your understanding of Jesus' healing then and now?

3. Next to the Holy Spirit, the Holy Scriptures are the greatest source of God's anointing available to you. What might happen if you devote yourself daily to really soaking in the Word, opening your heart and mind to its transforming power? Reflect on what God says in Hebrews 4:12; James 1:21; Acts 20:32; and Romans 1:16 as you answer.

PRACTICAL APPLICATION

But be ye doers of the word, and not hearers only, deceiving your own selves.
— James 1:22

1. Who do you know that is bound by a stronghold in their thinking? What practical steps can you take to get them near the anointing of God?

2. When was the last time you experienced a manifestation of God's anointing and you knew He was moving upon you? What took place when that happened?

3. If you can't remember the last time you flowed in the anointing of God, ask Him — the Great Anointer — to pour out a fresh anointing on you (*see* Psalm 23:5; 92:10). Not only will *you* be supernaturally refreshed, but you will become a source of refreshing for others!